THE SOLIS BLUEPRINT

A IN-DEPTH GUIDE ON HOW TO ACHIEVE GREATER HEIGHTS IN YOUR JOB HUNT

Quinn Scarlett & Rusin Andonov

Contents

- INTRODUCTION ... 2
  - Let's get started ... 4
- GETTING THE INTERVIEW ... 8
  - Sourcing Job Opportunities ... 9
  - The Warm-Lead and Warm-Email Approach ... 9
  - The Cold Email Approach (And How to Actually Do It!) ... 11
  - Finding Jobs in the Sea of Postings ... 13
  - Refine Your LinkedIn to Increase Your Chances ... 13
  - The Resume ... 17
    - FORMAT ... 18
    - SECTIONS ... 19
    - The One-Pager ... 20
    - The Two-Pager ... 20
    - The One-Pager ... 25
  - The Cover Letter ... 28
    - FORMAT ... 31
    - Letterhead to Recruiter ... 31
    - Introductory Statement ... 32
    - Experience Paragraphs ... 33
    - Concluding Statement ... 35
- THE INTERVIEW: BASICS ... 37
  - Charisma, Confidence, and Character (The 3 'C's) ... 38
  - Body Language, Eye-Contact ... 42
  - Dress for Success ... 44
- Conversational and Resume Focused Interviews ... 45
  - The Storyboard Method ... 46
  - How To Answer The 'Classic' Questions in Conversational Interviews ... 50
  - Tell us about yourself? ... 50
  - Tell us about your most recent job? ... 52
  - Why should we hire you? ... 53
  - How To Answer The 'Casual' Questions ... 55
- Behavioural Interviews ... 57
  - Preparation ... 58
  - The STAR Method ... 60
  - Deal-Sealing Methods ... 62
  - Multi-Pot Answers ... 63
- Case Interviews ... 65
  - Overview ... 66
  - Expectations and What Firms Look For ... 66
  - THE CASE ... 67
  - Core questions to memorize: ... 67
  - CCC (Customer, Company, Competition) ... 67
  - Various Frameworks ... 68
  - Case Structure and Approach ... 69
- Concluding Remarks ... 70

THE SOLIS
BLUEPRINT

INTRODUCTION

I'm happy you're here.
My name is Quinn Scarlett, alongside my colleague, Rusin Andonov, and we are so excited to provide you with the tools you need to arrive at your dream job.

The contents of this comprehensive crash course are not something novel, unique, or ground-breaking. We're not going to pretend like they are either. In fact, the "science" and art of interviewing have been exhaustively studied, researched, and developed over the past century. People with various degrees have laboured over ways to condense interviewing into a formulaic approach that can be replicated across all types of interviews, industries, and scenarios.

With their toolkits of psychometric analyses and behavioural measurements, MBAs, PhDs, and numerous professionals have written thousands of pages of books and papers trying to distill this unique social interaction down to something that can be copied and pasted.

If you were to type in 'Interview Prep' on Amazon, you would be met with thousands of options that would guide you through answering interview questions to mold to the frame of whatever is to come down the pipeline of your thirty minutes in the hot seat. From the infamous Case Study questions that you will inevitably get from Consulting Firms to the Resume and "Fit" style questions that a Law Firm may pose to the rigid behavioural questions that can come from any employer. YouTube will have the tutorials, Twitter will have the threads, and LinkedIn will have the inspirational posts. The resources are all there.

These resources are great for providing the base foundation for your professional journey. Heading into an interview without being equipped with the foundational tools such as framing and storytelling would be like running into a battle without any gear on. As crucial as these resources are, they are useless without refinement and utilization. These Amazon resources are all missing direct connection, guidance, and mentorship from two individuals who have amassed nearly 75

THE SOLIS BLUEPRINT

interviews in our professional journeys.

It doesn't matter how many professional Harvard Business School books or papers you have read on interview prep: **if you are not able to present yourself authentically, confidently, and create an impactful narrative that you can weave into any question, you are going to be at a disadvantage over your competitors!**

Throughout this document, we are not going to be reinventing the wheel. However, we will be adding a few more spokes in the wheel so that you can hit the ground as strong and ready as possible. This course will teach you how to exude confidence, rewrite scripts in your head that hold you back, connect with any interviewer across the table from you, and most importantly, handle any question that is quite literally thrown your way.

We want to establish a baseline understanding of what needs to be done for you to enter and leave an interview, ensuring the highest likelihood of a second interview and, even more ideally, the job or admissions offer, independent of your grades and your transcript.

This document will go over the fundamentals that the tried-and-true Amazon books will provide, but with a more esoteric twist. In interview prep, things that often go overlooked include psychology, spirituality, and personal growth. For example, the moment you determine that you are underqualified or out of your weight class before an interview is the second you have lost the job. This guide will be running through affirmations, scripts, self-talk and new psychological lenses for you to adapt to skyrocket the chances of your success.

We will then progress to the basics of each type of interview you can expect depending on the career path you can anticipate. Each of these industries is notorious for structuring its interviews in a particular way. Again, not reinventing the wheel but rather providing you with some new lenses and additional practices that you can adopt to maximize your chances of success. We intend to

THE SOLIS BLUEPRINT

supplement the swath of pre-existing information with techniques that have landed us both high-level jobs in our industries.

Lastly, and arguably most impactful, is the mentorship program. Should you finish the document and decide you want to work one on one with us, we will provide that opportunity for you. Both Rusin and I have made arrangements in our lives as law students and consultants to take in clients who want to level up. Our mentorship and coaching program provides weekly calls, planning, strategy, networking
tactics, resume and cover letter building, and personalized development exclusively for you and your unique career needs. The tools are the first step. If you don't practice and implement them in mock settings, source the right network, or learn how to leverage connections, you will get eaten by your competitors. I have made this mistake.

If this sounds like something you could benefit from, keep reading. I only wish I had a resource and mentorship like this before my professional pursuits to prevent me from making mistakes.

Let's get started.

You're probably wondering what our qualifications are, and why you should spend a second longer reading anything we have to say absent four or five professional degrees beside our names. My name is Quinn, I'm from Ontario, Canada. For the past eight years, I have been on quite the journey to find my professional, personal, and spiritual footing.

In high school, I learned the importance of professionalism, networking, getting comfortable interacting with people in powerful positions, and how to hold myself comfortably in a conversation. I happened to be a "Student Trustee" of my school board. Essentially, representing every student in my geographical region at the board level alongside superintendents and adult trustees. I regularly

THE SOLIS BLUEPRINT

interacted with individuals in positions of power, and I loved every second of it. Being a 17-year-old and being thrust into a room of people who are responsible for drafting every piece of policy that comes out for a school board instilled how to listen, learning how to speak up, and learning how to exercise basic professional skills such as my posture, diction, inflection, and charisma.

I went to a highly-ranked University in Canada, the same University that Elon Musk went to—Queen's University—for a degree in Biology with the ambitions of becoming a physician. The four years of my degree exposed me to numerous forms of extra-circulars that allowed me to regularly practise my interview skills. I can confidently say that I garnered exposure to case-study interviews, behavioural style interviews, and conversational interviews. My interviewing came to an apex in the final year of my degree. I secured one of three positions at an International NGO in South America. This was one of the first memorable moments in my professional career, and I felt that I had an excellent knack for interviewing.

Fast forward to writing this now, I am not a physician, nor am I in medical school, but rather a law student at a highly ranked law school in Canada. Being a law student aspiring to work at a reputable firm requires a trial by fire, with formalized and structured recruits being the only official door into the best firms in the country. These strict, ruthless processes leave no space for emotional grievances. Firms will spit you out of the process at the first sign of incompatibility or incompetency. Through many learned failures, I landed a job at a highly reputable firm in the city I reside in, presumably having to oust several hundred other candidates for my position. In reflection of this feat, I have realized quite a few essential dogmas that I hope to share throughout this document.

In counting my interview experiences, I have been through nearly 30 formal interviews, from the NGO sector to the public sector to the private sector. I have observed what sticks, what stands out, and what secures a recruiter's interest. In contrast, I have experienced what ruins an interview. What makes a recruiter think you're full of it, what phrases, actions, and mannerisms will push a recruiter away, and what will guarantee you never get a callback.

THE SOLIS BLUEPRINT

I want to make sure you get the distillation of nearly a decade of trial and error in the form of crystalized, market-ready success. My closest attempt at a formula that can be framed across any form of an interview that you encounter.

Another welcome to everyone seeking to better themselves and take their interview and career skills to the next level, my name is Rusin.

I currently work within the IT consulting industry following the completion of my undergraduate and graduate degrees at the University of Florida. I'm from Tampa, Florida. I have grown and developed my professional and leadership skills over the past seven years through my career, education, and professional organization experience.

Everything kicked off in high school for me. My involvement in the International Bachelorette program and Student Government allowed me to build the foundation for communicating and negotiating with individuals in positions of power. I planted the seeds of a growing network that later became one of my most powerful assets as a professional. Through my involvement in a leadership role within student government, I built a framework and toolset for communicating, actively listening, and interacting with professionals and individuals at higher levels with more experience. This allowed me to develop negotiation and communication skills that I could leverage and refine as my experience grew. It was an invaluable experience as later I later felt comfortable in situations of interviews and presentations while calmly carrying myself in discussion with professors, recruiters, and experienced professionals. With confidence, I can say that my exposure to these experiences in high school provided the backbone for me to be successful as early on as possible in my professional career.

Moving on to my collegiate experience, I attend the University of Florida, which is ranked #5 in public universities within the US and top 30 overall. During my attendance, I developed and sharpened technical and soft skill experience to a level that prepared me to tackle the industry. I had numerous experiences that nurtured my professional networking, interview, and resume skills throughout my four years.

THE SOLIS
BLUEPRINT

During my first two years, I involved myself in various leadership organizations within the business college, eventually taking on leadership roles and conducting interview processes myself. Further, I interned every summer from my freshmen to senior year in graduate school, with the invaluable experience of studying and working abroad in Dublin, Ireland during the summer before my sophomore year. However, the most pivotal experience I had was interning and eventually full-time consulting with a Big Four upon my graduation. This provided me with the best foundation for my career and understanding and exposure to and professional services multistage interview process, including case-study interviews.

Nearly three years following my graduation and two years within my professional career as a consultant, I now understand the process and what is required and expected of candidates. Along with my technical experience with clients, I have participated in recruiting and education committees. I have gained further knowledge of what it takes to be a successful professional alongside the nuances and skills required to present myself in the most unique manner.

I have been through numerous formal interviews, from professional organizations to professional public services firms to start-ups. Like my partner Quinn, I have absorbed and distilled the most valuable and efficient practices and habits to employ to make oneself a standout successful client. I look forward to building on my arsenal of tools and skills as my career progresses.

As we continue our professional and individual journeys, we seek to provide a helping hand to those who seek to avoid many of the trials and errors we experienced. As young professionals, our goal is to empower a better working world, helping those who find themselves struggling and confused in finding direction and success in taking a step towards their desired leadership or career roles. We invite you to join us in collaboratively and proactively assisting you with the steps needed to enable you to feel powerful, confident, and capable in successfully overcoming the recruitment process for your dream role.

GETTING THE INTERVIEW

THE SOLIS BLUEPRINT

This section will cover an area that I believe is seriously neglected in all forms of interview prep, which is the actual process of securing an interview. Most Amazon Best Sellers regarding interview strategy operate on the crucial presumption that you have an interview lined up. Before we dive into interview specifics, let's ensure that you know how to maximize your chances of landing an interview.

Sourcing Job Opportunities

Many of you reading this may be in college or university at the moment with a clear idea of where you want to end up. The benefit of being in a post-secondary institution is the swath of job fair-esque events that allow you to meet and hear directly from recruiters who are hiring.

Take advantage of every. Single. Networking. Event that you can get your hands on. Whether that is an organized job fair from your faculty, your friends' faculties, or even a neighbouring school. More often than not, they're free and they have free food. Usually, you can keep tabs on these events through Facebook, but word of mouth is often a good place. I am such a proponent of these events because one of, if not the most important things you can do as an undergraduate student is to BUILD YOUR NETWORK.

The Warm-Lead and Warm-Email Approach

Building your network will be the most monumental thing you can do to secure your interviews in the future. The old adage, "it's about who you know," is alive and well. If you can hear about a job before it goes public online through a friend or contact who works at a firm, you have much more of a headstart to prepare your materials. Suppose you can get a referral into a company through a connection that already works there. In that case, you have an advantage that the general public does not. Do not feel bad or guilty about leveraging these nepotic springboards. The world has, does, and will continue to operate in this fashion.

THE SOLIS BLUEPRINT

The next method you can use to source a job opportunity is the warm-email approach—not to be confused with the cold email— which is regularly utilized. In this approach, you get a referral (ideal situation) from a friend to connect you in an email, virtually introducing you and said connection at the company of interest. You and said connection "take the reins" from the email thread and converse separately. Here is where you sell yourself in a few sentences and inquire about setting up a brief coffee chat to further discuss the company and any potential work opportunities. An example email is attached below, one that I have personally used:

Hi **Name**,

I hope that this email finds you well and that you've had a restful weekend.

As [PERSON THAT CONNECTED YOU] so kindly mentioned, My name is [YOUR NAME], and I'm strongly interested in the prospect of working at [COMPANY]. I'm very curious to learn more about the scope of your work in the [practice area or group]. I'm wondering if we could talk either tomorrow or Tuesday between 12:00 and 3:00 pm for a brief coffee chat for me to learn a little more.

Please let me know if that works for you or if you have another preferred time, and I'd be happy to send over a Teams link for us to chat.

All my best,

YOUR NAME

THE SOLIS BLUEPRINT

It doesn't need to be glamorous, excessive, or over the top. What matters is you show up and get your name on the radar. The person who connects you to a lead within a company can be a current or past employee or merely a friend of the lead. Again, you should see the pattern here of the importance of getting noticed and getting on the radar, independent of how you do it.

The Cold Email Approach (And How to Actually Do It!)

Cold calling, cold emailing, cold leads, etc. The word 'cold' before any verb pertaining to sales or job hunting indicates that the individual/company/lead you are about to contact has zero affiliation or pre-emptive connection to you and your motives. You're going in without a warmup or introduction. You're making your own starting lane. You're making your own luck.

When I did sales in South America for a year, we were taught about the finicky nature of cold leads. Their ambiguous nature and outcomes often resulted in them being dealt with less than our pile of warm leads, as warm leads often lead to better results. The exciting thing about cold leads is you never know how far they can take you. Like any form of rejection, be that a shot at your crush or the shot at your dream job, the worst that will happen is a flat no. On the inverse, the best thing that can happen with a cold lead is the great unknown. Sometimes a cold lead can literally flip into the most remarkable success story of your life, so don't knock or doubt their validity.

An excellent cold email is always going to take the same skeletal approach:

1. Introduction and summary of yourself
2. What you are looking for
3. Why you are qualified and why you should get it

THE SOLIS
BLUEPRINT

The introduction to yourself should be kept to two sentences max. Short, rapid-fire elevator pitch. Cut to the chase and skip the buttery, flowery language. State what you're inquiring about. The earlier in your email, the better. Here is an example email template that you're free to try out and alter to match your writing flare:

Good evening, [Name of Cold Lead],
I'm hoping that this email finds you well and that you've been able to enjoy the nice weather as of late. [ADD IN SOME GENERAL COMMENTARY IF YOU SEE FIT]

*My name is [Your Name], and I am a current **[whatever you are]** student at the University [Your School]*

*I am emailing you today to express my interest in working for [Corporation] for the upcoming **summer**. The civil litigation work done at your firm strongly resonates with me, particularly the birth injury/medical malpractice realms. [Add something about their work that interests you]*

*Given my extensive involvement in civil litigation on the Pro Bono Student Society at my school, alongside my extensive work abroad with clients of all walks of life, I am confident I would be an excellent fit for your firm this **summer** and would love for the opportunity to garner any experience working alongside skilled civil litigators. [something about your related experience]*

In this email you will find attached my cover letter expressing my interest, my resume, and my grade transcript. I would be very keen to chat over a phone call to go over my background and documents should you have any questions

Wishing you a great rest of your week, and I look forward to hearing back from you.

All my best,

THE SOLIS BLUEPRINT

You can find tons of these templates online. The most important thing is that you adhere to my framework in structuring your cold emails. Keep it concise and confident, and don't overwrite. In our mentorship programs, part of our documentation editing will be to help you craft the perfect cold-email template.

Finding Jobs in the Sea of Postings

One of the most significant advantages of living in a world of social-media saturation is the increase in exposure that we have to opportunities all around the world. Some that we may have never known existed before the dawn of the internet. Looking for jobs is easier than ever, with employment aggregates such as LinkedIn Jobs, Indeed, Monster, etc. The list goes on.

As great as these services are, a consistent problem I ran into when using them was the complete over-saturation of applicants. Within hours of a LinkedIn job posting, one can see that well into the triple digits of individuals have not only viewed the posting but applied. I was always left wondering how I would land a job through this method and whether or not my application would even be read.

There is a method to this madness, and it can be broken down into a few steps that can rev up your shot at getting hired. Out of all the provided services, no service is more unique than LinkedIn. Unlike traditional e-hiring platforms where you uploaded your resume and waited for a company that liked your credentials to give you a shot, any job application you submit on LinkedIn is canvassed on the backdrop of your entire LinkedIn profile. Ensure that you make this work in your favour.

Refine Your LinkedIn to Increase Your Chances

Many of these online services weed out applicants automatically before a recruiter will even look at the pile of prospects. This "trimming the fat" process often goes to the few quantifiable things on an online profile or resume that a robot can quickly sift through. Usually, that is the skills section of your resume and the skills section of your LinkedIn. The solution to this is to have as many LinkedIn Skills listed on your

THE SOLIS BLUEPRINT

profile as possible that match the requirements or scope of the job you are seeking. You can bang off a few of them that are almost guaranteed to satisfy a checkmark, such as Microsoft Office, Public Speaking, Client & Customer Service, Research, etc. What happens when the robot is done with the trimming and your application is left in the pile? Time to make sure you look the part. Optics and first impressions are everything. You need to take your LinkedIn profile seriously so that recruiters take you seriously. I'm not going to harp too long on the things that I'm sure you have read and know about, but let's go over some basics:

1. **Make sure you don't have a selfie for a LinkedIn photo.** Go the extra length and look good and get a professional headshot done. Some of these can be done for as cheap as $30. I guarantee you that you know one friend with a nice camera or the newest iPhone that can take these shots for you.
2. **Make sure your summary is up to date and effective.** A good LinkedIn summary can be the make or break whether or not a recruiter wants to give you a chance. A good summary captures who you are, gives you a great sale, and makes you sound interesting. I like to look at summaries as the balance between two speeches. The first type of speech is the speech you give about your friend who you are trying to wingman. The second speech is the one that you have to give about a friend that you are introducing as a keynote speaker. The sweet spot is somewhere in between those two speeches. Here is mine below:

About

Second-Year Law Student at the University of Ottawa with an immense amount of international experience in the private and public sector. Fueled with an unparalleled passion and supported with a highly dynamic toolkit of leadership & executive skills.

With a notable ability to energize and galvanize teams, I can actualize goals, manifest results, and continually redefine what is considered attainable across different environments.

I am drawn to an array of advocacy work, with considerable experience in realms such as addiction, male well-being, and mental health.

Confident in leading and navigating the realms of a sales dynamic, team dynamic, and finding harmonious solutions across language and cultural barriers.

Passionate about the intersections of international affairs, health, technology, and politics.

THE SOLIS
BLUEPRINT

3. The third, and the boldest suggestion by far, is to **cold email the recruiter from the company and ask to set up a brief call to discuss particulars about the job.** If you can get a face to a name for the person combing through the pile of applications, your chances of landing the job have skyrocketed. Usually, you can find the recruiter's name through the job posting itself or by looking at the company directory. If that is not available, search "company name + location + Director of HR" on Google and you should get some good leads on who to contact.

   For example, I see a job at IBM Chicago that I am interested in. I know that it's for a career in their legal department, but that is all I can really see on the LinkedIn post aside from the job description and requirements. I know that this competition pool will be heavy, so I want to increase my chances of getting an interview and putting my name on the map. I discover who the HR Manager is and fire off an email in a quick search. As a quick test, think of local companies in your city and test yourself to see if you can discover who the HR Director of each respective company and department is.

4. **Be active on LinkedIn to the point where a recruiter should be able to look at your profile and see your recent activity.** Actively engage with the content your connections create, go out on a limb, and start creating your own content. You want to make sure that you've crossed the coveted 500+ connections mark at the minimum to ensure that you look like you're well connected and know what you're doing.

5. **LinkedIn Premium.** Use the free trial whenever you are offered it, and when you go to cancel, they will try to offer it to you for 50% off. If you are actively hunting and hungry for a job, LinkedIn Premium will allow you to see the job postings that you are "most qualified" for based on the skills that I mentioned in point number one. Further proof that so much of this process is robotized. Make sure you take advantage of the tools at your disposal and conquer the Robot.

THE SOLIS BLUEPRINT

6. **Cold Email/Message employees that work at the company of interest.** This is one of my favourite strategies that I regularly did during my law firm recruits. Let's go back to my IBM Chicago example. I know that I'm gunning for a spot in their legal department for the summer, so I use LinkedIn to discover who else works in said department. After narrowing down a list of employees, try to spot those you think you would connect with best. Look for alumni schools, fraternities or sororities, or even common interests. This will significantly increase your chances of converting your cold email into a coffee chat. I've used very similar templates for my cold email coffee chat requests, which you can see below.

> *Good morning, Mr. [NAME]*
>
> *I hope this email finds you well. My name is [YOUR NAME], I'm a [PROGRAM/STUDENT] at [SCHOOL], and I'm thrilled to be applying for a summer position at [COMPANY]*
>
> *In preparation for my interviews, your profile, and particularly, your work with M&As and commercial law more generally, caught my attention, and I was wondering if you would be willing to field some questions I have for you at some point next week?*
>
> *I would love to get a more authentic idea and understanding of the firm culture and how it has been working in commercial law at [COMPANY] in particular.*
>
> *If you have any time to chat Monday or Tuesday of next week for 15 minutes, please let me know, and I'll be happy to make whatever works.*
>
> *Looking forward to hearing from you, and all my best.*
>
> *YOUR NAME*

Now that you have a better idea of optimizing your chances of getting a LinkedIn posting, let's move on to the crucial documents required for any other posting— be that Indeed, an internal posting, or a formal recruit. Your Resume and Cover Letter.

THE SOLIS BLUEPRINT

The Resume

I wrote this book wanting to stay in my wheelhouse. The informational market for resume advice is highly oversaturated and confusing for newcomers to the job market. One quick Google search and you'll be whisked away to forums of people claiming that their resume template is the holy grail of all templates.

I knew from the beginning that I wanted to avoid getting too far in the reeds with resume advice. However, there are pieces of cornerstone advice that I want to give that will be crucial in ensuring your success. Therefore, we will ensure you have the foundational boxes ticked before you go trigger happy on the job applications. Resumes are critical in getting you through the door, and this goes for law, consulting, finance, and med-school. It doesn't matter how strong you are of an interviewer; if your resume is part of the pile that gets trimmed, well, better luck next year.

Before I showcase a good resume template, it is essential that we walk through the "must-haves" of resume building blocks, independent of the field you are pursuing.

THE SOLIS BLUEPRINT

FORMAT

The age-old question of font, spacing, size, and margins. Honestly, anyone who even bothers to touch margins is someone who doesn't know what they're talking about. I can put my right hand on the bible and attest that I cannot think of one time in my life aside from graphic designs in which I had to change the margins. Don't touch them and leave your standard document the size when you open it. If you happen to be the person that cares about margins, make sure that they are between 8mm and 16mm.

Moving on to font, and what I am about to say is entirely a personal preference, but I have heard down the grapevine that it is a silent industry preference: Times New Roman gets the job done. Don't get creative and explorative with your font choice and choose Calibri or Arial. You are here to make a statement about your work experience and why you are an excellent candidate, not flex the left side of your brain. That time will come in your interviews.

For font size, choose an 11. I know that 12 is the standard for assignments, but we are only limited to two (2) pages, so you want to make everything count. Every. Single. Word. Counts on your resume, and I will continually return to this point.

On to your personal information—a little trick that I learned to save space on my resume during my first year of law school was to put my contact/personal information in the document's heading. Simply double-click the dead white space at the top center of your naked word document, and the option to fill in a header should appear. My header structure and format are below. I used a size 16 font for my name to stand out and a size 12 on the contact details.

QUINN MICHAEL FOSTER
10 Summer Street, Toronto, ON, K1J 1H4 | 123-456-XXXX | your.email@urschool.ca

First Page Header EDUCATION

THE SOLIS BLUEPRINT

Looking at the word "EDUCATION" above, you will understand how I "title" my sections in my resume. 11-point font, Times New Roman, but capitalized and bolded to draw attention and differentiate section from substance. Below each section, you will want to add in a thick black line to go across the entire document to "square" off your sections. See below. If you have a hard time with that, try making a 1x1 table or experimenting with underscores to achieve the desired effect.

PROFESSIONAL EXPERIENCE
_____

SECTIONS

This is easily the most contentious area of resume building. I want to apologize if I am about to add another perspective to resume structuring to the existing pile you've already seen. There is no correct answer, though there are objectively better formats than others. Let's get this out of the way right now. I HATE, and I mean, I REALLY hate seeing resumes that decide to put an "objectives" section. Have you ever heard of a cover letter? If you have that in your resume, I strongly suggest you take it out, and at least at the minimum, if you are going into law school. Specific industries may have that as a norm, such as managerial consulting, however,

A well-formatted resume usually flows in a variation that is like the following:

> Overview
> Education
> Awards & Publications
> Work & Volunteer Experience
> Languages and Skills

You must check the industry standard for your stream of applications. For example, it is customary to submit a two-page resume in law if not expected. No less, no more. The research will show that various consulting firms are looking for a nice, crisp one-page resume that embodies a similar flow to the sections I listed above. We will unpack these different page formats individually.

THE SOLIS BLUEPRINT

The One-Pager

Something that is highly contested is whether the one-pager resume is king. Like any good lawyer would say to you, the answer is that it depends. For consulting, finance, and managerial positions that you apply to with under 10 years of experience, the verdict seems to be that one-page resumes are the norm and preferred. However, the trend is constantly changing and is something you may want to check in for your desired industry.

If you opt for a one-page resume, a few formatting points need to be adhered to. The first is that you can potentially get away with a smaller font like 10.5, given how pressed you may be for space. The header suggestion I mentioned earlier will really come in handy to free up some space for you.

The most important piece of advice on a one-pager is to make sure that when (not if) you are writing your bullet point descriptions, you are being highly selective and strategic with your descriptions. If you were one of the best former employees, OWN that and gloss your language up to be "positioned myself to be one of the most effective employees out of a team of _____, generating over ___% growth in ___ months." Talk about yourself in a way that your mother would at your funeral.

A great one-pager resume example is below:

The Two-Pager

I really like this resume format, mainly because it is the one I am most comfortable with; however, it also allows you to insert more elaborative descriptions of your work experience. Before using the two-page format, it is strongly suggested that you research the "industry" standards for what you're applying for. This is an excellent choice if you're like me and enjoy writing in dramatic, powerful language.

THE SOLIS BLUEPRINT

The most important thing that you try to adhere to with this structure is prioritizing your most impressive or recent job experience. Not all your work experience should have five bullet points of description; however, the first job you have listed under the Work Experience section should be the eye-catcher.

The resume that I used, though highly redacted for obvious reasons, is as follows:

EDUCATION

Juris Doctor (J.D).   2020-Present
University of YOUR CITY, Faculty of Law, ON
- English Common Law Program
- 2023 Candidate

Bachelor of Science (Honours), Class of 2019   2015-2019
YOUR University, Faculty of Arts and Science – Department of Biology, YOUR CITY, ON
- Major in Biology

AWARDS & PUBLICATIONS

University of XXXX – Faculty of Common Law   **2021**
- Achieved the highest mark in **XXXXX** – Commercial Law for the Fall 2021 semester.

The Lawyer's Daily   2021
- My analytical piece on the overlaps of privacy law and artificial intelligence and the investigation into the RCMP's utilization of facial recognition software: Privacy Laws, Artificial Intelligence

The XXXX Journal   **2018**
- Self-authored investigative article in The Journal titled: Male Mental Health

The XXXX Alumni Review   **2018**
- Interviewed in full-length feature article in the Fall 2018 Publication of The XXXX Alumni Review - link

THE SOLIS BLUEPRINT

PROFESSIONAL EXPERIENCE

Summer Intern & Current Part-Time Student   2021-Present
Law Canada, Toronto, ON
- Worked on array of civil litigation matters alongside XXXXX. Responsibilities included preparing memoranda, affidavits, pleadings, mediation briefs and aiding in document review.
- Aided in the preparation of documents for appellate cases at Ontario Court of Appeal.
- Used a wide range of legal research tools including AI-driven software, Alexsei.
- Prepared and published articles for firm website and The XXXX Daily.

Associate Editor   2020-Present
The XXXX Law Review, University of XXXX, ON
- Responsible for the executive editing of legal publications and scholarship, ensuring accurate grammar, syntax, and clarity while regularly collaborating with Senior Editors on projects.
- Responsible for mentoring Assistant Editors through the XXX Mentorship program.
- Serving on Special Projects Committee, helping coordinate research colloquiums and events

International Associate   2019-2020
XXXX International, Lima, Peru
- Managed a transnational portfolio of over 62 clients across Canada from Lima, Peru, and was directly responsible for Canadian expansion across several provinces.
- Increased the Canadian portfolio by over 290% in revenue in an eight-month period whilst securing numerous international partnerships in a fast-paced, multilingual work environment.
- Frequently aided in field projects within developing communities across Peru and Ecuador alongside local leaders through the construction of sustainable homes and education centers.
- Regularly consulted and worked alongside Indigenous community leaders in Lima.

THE SOLIS BLUEPRINT

President   2018-2019
Alma-Mater Society at XXXX University – XXXX Queens
- Spearheaded the largest NGO society at XXXX University, and 4th largest society overall.
- Managed a team of 15 executives and 72 general members across all universities in orchestrating large-scale fundraisers, conferences, and International Service-Learning Trips.

Director   2018-2019
XXXX for the Boys, Mental Health Network, XXXX, Ontario
- Led of one of the largest mental health advocacy bodies on campus, advocating on male mental health through campus funded research projects and
policy initiatives.
- Co-led and implemented campus-wide harm reduction programs, including Naloxone kit distribution, with the Alma Mater Society of XXXX and XXXX Public Health.

Research Assistant   2016-2019
XXXX University Department of Psychiatry & Department of Health Policy Studies, XXXX, ON
- Conducted research on the interconnections between gender, mental health, and substance misuse on three university campuses in Canada, under the supervision of Dr. XXX XXX.
- Led my own team of student researchers for the Canadian Centre for Substance Abuse and Addiction, implementing media campaigns and surveys targeting sentiments on binge drinking

International Delegate   2018
AIESEC International, Requena, Province of Valencia, Spain
- Served as an international delegate for AIESEC, teaching and administering English and Science classes at an international summer school in rural Spain in a multicultural environment.

THE SOLIS BLUEPRINT

EXTRACURRICULARS

Director of Events — 2021-Present
Elephant in the Room – XXXX Common Law, Mental Health Advocacy Team
- Senior executive member of largest mental health advocacy body at XXXX Law.

Student Triathlete — 2017-2019
XXXX Varsity Triathlon - Club Member, XXXX, ON

Lifeguard and Swim Instructor — 2017-2019
XXXX Department Aquatics and the Town of XXXXX

Head of First Aid and Emergency Response — 2017
Enrichment Studies Unit Program – XXXX University, XXXX, ON

LANGUAGES AND INTERESTS
- Fluent in English and Advanced Proficiency in Spanish (C1 Level - reading, writing, oral)
- Triathlete and long-distance runner. Have completed the David Goggins 4x4x48 ultra-marathon.
- Host of the mental health podcast, 'XXXX' Garnered over 1,500 streams.
- Currently managing a mental health clothing line under the XXXX Project through Etsy.
- Convinced that no TV show will ever surpass Ozark. Terrible at golf but will always say yes to it.

Think what you will of this format, but it is well known, respected, and widely used. I really like the straightforwardness of this resume style, and like how it gives me the room to expand on numerous different areas of my professional and personal experience. This is not a risky resume style, and will not be off-putting to any reader.

THE SOLIS BLUEPRINT

The One-Pager

Something that is highly contested is whether the one-pager resume is king. Like any good lawyer would say to you, the answer is that it depends. For consulting, finance, and managerial positions that you apply to with under 10-15 years of experience, the verdict seems to be that one-page resumes are the norm and preferred. However, the trend is constantly changing and is something you may want to check in for your desired industry. Generally, in the consulting industry, the one-pager resume is taken up a notch with the level of attention to detail regarding wording, quantitively presenting your impact, and outlining integral technical knowledge. Many often struggle with the limitations of a one-page resume. While it may be difficult to best present all of your experience and skills, this limitation is actually a powerful tool in presenting your value most effectively. The one-pager embodies the saying "less is more,' perfectly and strives to force the writer to include only the most essential details, which effectively is what a resume is all about.

First and foremost, your one-page resume should be formatted professionally. Your current/alumni degree program's resume template is often a great place to start. The Wharton format and the Harvard format are examples that will work well for the foundation of your one-page resume. Generally, from experience and widely expected formatting seen across Fortune 500 companies, we recommend having four to five sections within your one-page resume: Education, Professional Experience, Technical Skills, Leadership/Involvement, and Additional Information. We recommend not including an Overview section unless you have professional experience of more than 10 years spanning across a variety of roles and levels.

The most important piece of advice on a one-pager is to make sure that when (not if) you are writing your bullet point descriptions that you are being highly selective and strategic with your descriptions. Put your achievements in the spotlight, OWN your value and gloss your language up to be "positioned myself to be one of the most effective employees out of a team of _____,'

THE SOLIS BLUEPRINT

generating over ___% growth in ___ months." Embody your best salesperson mindset and promote your skills, achievements, and experience as if you are trying to sell yourself as the product and what value that would present to the employer. Do not hesitate to slightly exaggerate as long as it is within the context and truthfulness of your actual experience.

We have found the most successful one-pager resumes to have three critical traits that allow you to present your value in the most conscience manner.

MAKE EVERY WORD COUNT
- Use buzzwords specific to the industry or role you are looking to apply to quantify your achievements and impact through short, action-oriented bullet points.
- Remove all possible filler words.

FOCUS ON CLEAN AND CONCISE FORMATTING
- Try to keep each bullet point to a line or less.
- Use consistent fonts, size, and spacing between headers, body, and bullet points.
- Present everything in a chronological order

CONSISTENTLY UPDATE AND REFRESH
- Revisit your resume for updates for every new role you apply to.
- When possible, consistently seek feedback from colleagues or friends.
- Be creative and include details that make you unique

View a great one-pager resume example for a two-to-three-year experienced consulting professional on the next page.

Michael Smith
+1 (123) 456-7891 | smith.michael@gmail.com | www.linkedin.com/in/michael.smith

EDUCATION
University of Florida, Hough Graduate School of Business **May XXXX**
Master of Science in Information Systems and Operations Management (MSISOM) Gainesville, FL
- Track: Business Intelligence and Data Analytics

University of Florida, Warrington College of Business **May XXXX**
Bachelor of Science in Business Administration, Information Systems Gainesville, FL
- Study Abroad in Dublin, Ireland - Griffith College (May XXXX - Aug XXXX)

EXPERIENCE
Ernst & Young **August XXXX – Present**
Business Consulting Staff Tampa, FL
Serve clients in the Hospitality & Construction, Media & Entertainment, and Professional Firms and Services sectors to deliver value-driven solutions and results
- Evaluate the client's technology environment and business, execute in-depth assessments of the IT processes and risks
- Lead walkthroughs to access clients' IT applications and security to develop audit plan
- Communicate and manage meetings, follow-ups, and coordination with clients, building value driven relationships
- (Bullet Point 4)
- (Bullet Point 5)

Ernst & Young **June XXXX – August XXXX**
Risk Advisory Intern Tampa, FL
Provided excellent client service, working with clients and team members to meet project deliverables
- Acquired strong risk assessment and management skills by evaluating client's IT environments and business processes
- Managed walkthrough meetings by coordinating, taking notes, collecting evidence, and maintaining follow-up dialogue
- Utilized strong communication, management, and technical skills to foster valuable client relationships
- (Bullet Point 4)
- (Bullet Point 5)

Griffith College IT **May XXXX – August XXXX**
Data Analyst Intern Dublin, Ireland
Managed a data analytics and visualization project serving all levels of the college
- Leveraged Power BI and SQL to develop trackable live metrics for the seven major faculties
- Mapped databases, creating Entity Relationship Diagram (ERD) to establish multi-relational structure between databases
- Improved data retrieval efficiency significantly and established trackable KPIs to improve statistical forecasting
- (Bullet Point 4)
- (Bullet Point 5)

TECHNICAL SKILLS
Programming Languages: Python, Java, R **Business Intelligence Tools**: MS PowerBI, Tableau
Certifications: Certified Information Systems Auditor (CISA) **Databases**: ETL, SQL

LEADERSHIP & INVOLVEMENT
EY Tampa – Education Committee August XXXX - Present
UF Technology Case Competition Team August XXXX – December XXXX
Warrington Diplomats - *VP of Programming* May XXXX – May XXXX
International Programs Student Ambassador - *Content Committee Chair* September XXXX – May XXXX
Florida Leadership Academy April XXXX – May XXXX

THE SOLIS BLUEPRINT

The Cover Letter

The cover letter (CL) can be one of the most elusive and methodical aspects of securing a job. I have gruelled and slaved over 100 hours on my cover letters for a law recruit, and honestly, I still didn't feel it was enough time. I want you not to feel like you need to spend 100 hours whittling down a 500-word document to perfection and instead attack your CL with the focus and refinement that you know you need in little to no time.

Writing the "perfect" cover letter is all about having the utmost insight into who your employer is and the cookie-cutter requirements for the role you are applying for. Suppose you were applying for a job as a consultant and droned on about your time as a backpacker in Kilimanjaro. Here, most recruiters will ask what you're doing wasting their time. HOWEVER, if you can convert your experience in Kilimanjaro to be one that has beget you with the perfect arsenal of tools that make you the best consultant they have ever seen in their career. . . well, you're on to something. Let's dive a little deeper into that.

THE SOLIS
BLUEPRINT

You want to look at a cover letter not so much as a summary of your resume, but as a sales pitch about the **best transferable skills** your resume experiences have bestowed on you. From here, you **extend and mold** those skills to be directly applicable to the criterion and culture of the job you are applying for. Gone are the days that you use a generic cover letter for each job. You will be using a similar template for different jobs, but you must ensure that you are actively namedropping, referencing, and paying homage to the particular company you are applying for in your CL.

We're going to keep circling back to the Kilimanjaro example.

On its face, a recruiter may see you mention this in your CL and just see a hiking expedition. It may strike some people as you just being a spoiled applicant that likes to travel. While that may be true, you need to REDUCE the experience into its barebone skills & CONVERT those skills into a pitch that is molded directly to what the employer wants to see.

Let's do the reduction aspect together:
We started with a hiking expedition to Kilimanjaro that took two weeks. You therein developed the following skills that can be converted to the office environment:
- Problem solving (from navigating high-altitude, varying climates)
- Adaptability (see above)
- Tenacity and Grit (from climbing up one of the tallest mountains in the world while maintaining resolve and commitment)
- Ability to work under pressure
- Ability to focus in high stress
- Ability to see the bigger picture

THE SOLIS
BLUEPRINT

The list can literally go on, and it is all about how you choose to distill your unique experiences and apply them to the task at hand. Now, in case you are not someone who has climbed Kilimanjaro, or you are an applicant that worries that you don't have any "stand-out" experiences like some of your peers, this reduction and conversion formula can literally apply to any job, including something as simple as working at a fast-food joint.

- Ability to work long hours and maintain resolve
- Ability to service customers from all walks of life with professionalism
- Ability to work under immense pressure
- Ability to work in a dynamic team in a fast-paced environment

If I didn't tell you those skills are from working at Burger King, you would think those are pretty good skills. The thing is, they are. All experiences, except for sitting on your parent's couch in the basement, can be REDUCED AND CONVERTED into ANYTHING that a job is looking for. Stop selling yourself short and get after it.

In fact, I have seen a colleague of mine with a similar background (working at a Diner and local social group home for his undergraduate) land one of the highest paying firms in Canada. All without the unpaid internship in Vienna, all without the UN placement, all without the accolades and awards. Just a well-reduced and converted background that tells a damn good story. This gets into the next aspect of a good cover letter. What type of storyteller you are, and the story you choose to author.

THE SOLIS BLUEPRINT

FORMAT

Now that we know how to distill your experiences into distinct skill-based talking points, let's talk about formatting your cover letter.

First and foremost, your resume and cover letter often will (and should) be in the same font. I used Times New Roman for mine at a size 11, but a size 12 with fewer words will likely exude the same effect.

A solid cover letter will be in the range of 350-500 words. Any less, and you run the risk of coming off as too surface level, with not enough experience to bolster your candidacy. Anymore and you run the risk of demonstrating that you cannot summarize and distill critical information, which is not a good look for any jobs requiring any semblance of writing or presenting.

The most bareboned, skeletal format that I can suggest for your cover letter is the following:

> Letterhead to Recruiter (2 or 3 lines)
> Dear xxxx:
> Introductory Statement
> Experience 1 and Transferable Skills
> Experience 2 and Transferable Skills
> Experience 3 and Transferable Skills
> Concluding Statement

Let's go through these one by one.

Letterhead to Recruiter

It should be two- or three-lines absolute tops. You must know the first and last name of the individual reading your cover letter. Dig your absolute hardest to find this information, and even resort to people you have made connections to in the

THE SOLIS BLUEPRINT

firm to find this out. A cover letter directly addressed to an individual versus "The Hiring Manager" will already start on a more personable tone.

Here is what my letterhead would have looked like in the past:

> **Attn: Kerry Smith—Director of Recruitment**
> 111 Prince Street, Suite 4300
> Edmonton, MB, K1P 1J9

Really nothing else to say here. Some people will post five or six lines of information when it is really just taking up space from selling yourself. The fourth line you can add right above the bolded recruiter line is the actual name of the company, but if you have the name and address exactly then it is a defaulted presumption. If you want to play it safe, please do so.

Introductory Statement

Have you heard the adage that people make their opinion about you within the first three seconds? It's incorrect. People make their opinion up about you after less than a second. Recruitment is no exception, which is why the first readable sentences need to be succinct, powerful, and captivating.

Within three sentences, the recruiter should know who you are, what your deal is, and what you want from them. Period. You need to be coming out strong and aggressive here.

A few examples below, one that I have used that landed me a position in one of the most prestigious societies in my law school during my first year.

THE SOLIS BLUEPRINT

> Please accept this letter and its enclosures as my application for the _____ for the _____. Stemming from a background in biology and mental health policy development, I have diverse experiences in academic publications, project management and can serve as an effective team leader. Through numerous global experiences and significant time spent working for an NGO abroad, I have cultivated a strong foundation of communication skills that I hope to further through your organization. I believe you will find that my professional experience and calibre of work done make me a strong candidate to advance as an Associate.

This is all preferential, and in retrospect, I would change a few things and dial down the word count. I would classify this introductory statement as "alright." But you're more than alright; you're exceptional. Let's do that exercise together and make this even more succinct and direct. Remember, we are looking for 2-3 sentences max.

Converting the above to a more refined version, we're left with this:

> I am [YOUR NAME], a [STUDENT OF WHATEVER PROGRAM] and I am applying for the position of _____ at _____. Hailing from a background in biology and policy development, as well as spending a year working for an NGO abroad, I have cultivated a strong foundation of verbal and written communication skills that I hope to apply through a long-term position with _____.

BOOM! To the point baby. That's an attention grabber, at least more of an attention grabber than 'my name is Slim Shady, and I am applying for the position of a Junior Consultant at your firm.' You've just ensured that the rest of whatever you want to say gets read by the recruiter at a higher rate than Slim Shady. You've captivated and held their attention span for at least another paragraph.

Experience Paragraphs

Suppose you've managed to grab the attention from your introductory statement. In that case, your next task will be to convince the recruiter that you are the chosen one for the job they seek to fill. Doing this requires that you REDUCE and CONVERT

THE SOLIS BLUEPRINT

your best experiences into a story that illustrates why you are the perfect match for the job.

An excellent way to structure your experience paragraphs is to start by taking one of your experiences, thinking about the most convertible skills, and then highlighting what you were doing in the experience that allowed you to hone that skill. If you are applying to a position that values writing, research, and editing, such as a law job or analyst position, you may want to make your convertible skills from your experiences those which align with those values. Customer and client service is always a good experience and skill to highlight no matter which industry you are applying to.

Example:

> My previous work in [INDUSTRY: sales, customer service, finance, etc.] makes me an excellent candidate for this position. As an International Associate with [COMPANY] I routinely supported diverse projects and portfolios across the Canadian market. I most notably secured partnerships with public-private stakeholders throughout Canada to help subsidize expansion projects. By leveraging my relationships with clients, I increased my portfolio revenue by 290% in under a year, This position taught me how to produce quality work that matched the diverse needs of my clients and instilled the importance of community development, a value that I know is reflected at [COMPANY YOU ARE APPLYING TO].

Let's skeletonize this a little more into a structure that you can replicate with your experience:

1. Statement about former job #1 making you an excellent candidate.
2. Brief summary of former job and most notable accomplishments and responsibilities
3. Convertible skills that you learned and its reflection in the company you are applying to

THE SOLIS BLUEPRINT

You will want to replicate this for all three of your experience paragraphs. How you choose to transition between each paragraph is really a stylistic choice. Suppose you have a diverse range of experience with the corporate world and less experience with "soft" extra-curriculars. In that case, your cover letter may span three different paragraphs with three other corporate jobs. However, I would caution you against that. The art of cover letter writing requires you to strike the balance of a workhorse with the requisite qualities and skills for the job while showcasing that you are someone with interests and experience that span outside of the office. This is my opinion; others will caution you against this.

Remember the Kilimanjaro example? Mountaineering? That has nothing to do with working in an office per se. Still, the convertible skillset is arguably more powerful and more interesting than talking about your three different office jobs in three separate paragraphs. They're going to start sounding similar. My suggestion is to take an experience or experiences that are extra-curricular in nature and use those as your final paragraph. If you played on a competitive team or varsity team, you most certainly want to write about that. If you have a knack for presentations and public speaking, you'll want to write about that. If you were in hospitality and that is your expansive, non-corporate experience. . . write about that.

The real groove is to show you're the Dos Equis person. The individual with a colourful background that boils down to being the ideal candidate for the position. Someone who knows the importance of TIME MANAGEMENT, WORK-ETHIC, CLIENT-SERVICE, TEAMWORK, INITIATIVE, PROBLEM-SOLVING, and RESOLVE (hint, steal and use these buzzwords).

Concluding Statement

This is the make-or-break point. The section which can sway a recruiter who was fence-sitting in your favour or not. You want to close this statement with power and conviction. Let the person who is reading this know that you want them to make a long-term investment in you and your success. Convey that you are the ideal candidate that can provide long-term value. A symbiotic relationship of success.

THE SOLIS
BLUEPRINT

An excellent way to look at closing statements is a brief remark about your skills, boiled down into a few words, followed by a sentiment that touches on the long-term investment into your growth and future.

My closing statement that I used in my last recruit looked like this:

> I am confident that my transferable skills will make me a valuable asset to your team, not only for the summer, but for the long-term. My diverse experiences show that I am fully prepared for the demands of [INDUSTRY]. I have committed myself to a life of client-driven advocacy, and it is at [COMPANY] that I would like to live out that commitment. Thank you for your time and consideration— I look forward to hearing from you.

You want to tie it all together. A good tip is to mention the long-term commitment piece. Recruiters don't want to feel like they're spending all this time in your growth for you to springboard somewhere else (even if that's true). Demonstrating long-term interest is a great bonus and should be mentioned independently of your intentions. Make sure you distill your skillset down to something like "my transferable skills" or "diverse experiences in client-service/research/consulting/finance."

This concludes this chapter on how to bolster your chances of getting the interview. The market is hot right now and will likely be hot for the next few years. Everyone is fighting to get through the same bottleneck you're aiming for. Making sure you stand out with your words will ensure a higher chance of getting noticed, even if you feel like your experience is lacking. You have the power to reduce and convert being a fry cook to being the most diligent, hard-working team player that applies to the company of interest. Mold your words into weaponry. Take stock of the network of people that work at the company and get ready to sound sharp in your interview.

THE INTERVIEW: BASICS

THE SOLIS BLUEPRINT

THE INTERVIEW: BASICS

We've made it to the bread and butter of the book. The reason (I presume) that you sought the book in the first place: the interview. How to prepare, how to navigate, how to dominate. We'll be covering all of those goalposts in the coming pages. Before we do any of that, we're going to cover the skeletal underpinnings of interviews, be that consulting, law, finance, policy, medicine, etc.... the underpinning that remains consistent across all these interviews: you and your story.

The most enthralling thing about interviews is that you have the choice to become the screenwriter, producer, director, and actor in your own storyboard that you choose to curate for the recruiters. In no sense am I suggesting that you fabricate things. Rather, you will learn to prepare in a way that tells a narrative that allows you to answer any question thrown your way and truly stand out from your competition.

Before you even do that, you need to ensure that the place that you are projecting that storyline from is from a place of confidence and conviction. A flirtatious balancing point of charisma and humility. All of these things, independent of your personality type or being an introvert or extrovert, need to be in order before you implement any interviewing strategies. There is no point in reading off a gold-medal script, should you even have one, if you are a fumbling and blubbering ball of insecurity that will be immediately sniffed out by the most amateur recruiter. Words can be fabricated and spoken by anyone. Confidence and character are earned and built. Let's start there.

Charisma, Confidence, and Character (The 3 'C's)

The 3 Cs are overused societal buzzwords, diluting their impact and significance. Many people have incorrectly associated confidence with egocentrism, and charisma with superficiality. Though those two things can all go hand-in-hand depending on the individual. It is your job to discover and re-orchestrate the alignment of those qualities to have the best, most desirable balance and

THE SOLIS
BLUEPRINT

outcome for your career, relationships, and life more generally.

I want you to pause and reflect on the most charismatic person that you know in your life. What makes them that way? What objective qualities do you think to assign and ascribe the charismatic title over them? Is it the fact that their voice carries a room? They light up in conversation and find a connecting point with anyone they talk to? They can make the dullest of parties extravagant in mere minutes? The first google search of charisma will distill all of these examples into a few sentences: Dynamic Communication, Passion, Enthusiasm, and Positive Body Language.

If you are naturally introverted, some of these skills may require more finesse, but trust me, every person can be a dynamic and expressive communicator within the confinements of their personality. Your job is not necessarily to replicate someone else but rather to bring every fibre of your personality and existence to the highest vibrational plane possible so that you genuinely are the most authentic and energized version of yourself in an interview (and life, but that's for another time).

The first step to this is going back to the basics of social interactions. A good thought experiment that you can do is the following:

Picture you are in a three-way conversation. The second person in the triad is someone you know well, and the third is a complete stranger who also happens to know the second person you know. Your mutual friend excuses himself to go grab something, and you are left alone with the third person who you know nothing about. Does this scenario cause or create anxiety for you? Are you having racing thoughts picture or strategizing how you would go about navigating this situation? If you answered yes, we got some recalibration to do.

EVERY SINGLE PERSON you have a social interaction with, be that a janitor or a CEO, a complete stranger at a party, or your lifelong best friend, has more similarities to you than differences. Realize that the only reason you're more nervous talking to a corporate executive than the janitor is because of the mental compartment that

THE SOLIS
BLUEPRINT

you have placed that person into. The anxiety that you get with recruiters is similar. You look at and perceive them as a threat. These individuals are in front of you to decide your fate, and God forbid you make a mistake. Of course, reading this right now in the comfort of your home and not in an interview mode, you're likely to see these fears as irrational. Let's keep them that way.

The key to socialization is to first realize that any social anxiety that paralyzes you and makes your palms sweat is entirely self-imposed. The second you detach yourself from expectations and fear of judgment from others is the first step to unlocking your charismatic side (a side that every person truly has). Often, people restrict or limit the energetic or elevated authenticity within them out of fears of the judgment of others. Fears of coming off as too much, being too loud, annoying, over-bearing, etc. While self-awareness is also a fantastic thing to have to ensure you don't cross over into those realms, people are often too hesitant to allow themselves to come out of their shells. If there is a noticeable disconnect between who you are with your closest friends and loved ones and who you are in public or in an interview—it is your job to bridge that gap.

Your closest friends and loved ones are your closest friends and loved ones, likely because they **enjoy** and **appreciate** your raw, unabridged authenticity. Referring back to introverted and extroverted, I remain convinced that regardless of what category you fall into, you are still the most "loud" and "dynamic" when you feel the safest. You must try your hardest to let some of that "close-friend" energy that you let out at home seep through into your daily life. Just as recruiters can sniff disingenuity, they are also experts at detecting authenticity. If you can let your authentic energy shine (YOU KNOW YOU HAVE IT!), it will be easily detectable and set your interviews off on the right foot. Though recruiters want to ensure that you have the requisite skills and qualities that suit their job, they are also looking for your compatibility with their workplace, often dubbed the "fit."

Suppose you hide, shelter, or blunt your authentic side for the interview and say, get the job. In that case, it may feel more uncomfortable letting that side slowly come out into the light as your career unfolds. You want to ensure that you are yourself

THE SOLIS BLUEPRINT

from start to finish, and I say this with an asterisk. If "you" means naturally quiet, docile, and reserved, you need to ensure that your authentic, behind closed doors energy that your close friends get to see naturally seeps out. This may take some practice, but trust me, it's worth it.

Confidence and character are things that people have written extensively about, and I'm not here to reinvent the wheel. I'm not going to spend too long on this, but I will say this:

If you do not like who you are as a person, if you have low self-esteem, or loathe parts of who you are, it is of the utmost importance (more important than any consulting job you can ever get) that you learn to fall madly and deeply in love with all of who you are, including the worst parts of you. Once you can fully accept who you are within the tapestry of all your shortcomings and weaknesses, guilt and mistakes, failures and errors, you will be extremely close to the domain of authentic confidence.

Confidence, to me, is the state of knowing what you bring to the table. Knowing you are of immense value and worth, knowing you are desirable, that you excel in your domains of strength, that you can obtain things that you set your sights on, often better than other people around you. The most important tenant of confidence is knowing that you are outcome-independent— that you are independent of peoples' thoughts, opinions, projections and decisions about you. You know who you are at the end of the day.

However, what separates confidence from ego is knowing that all of these things have limits: that you aren't the best at what you do, that you are surrounded by more capable people than you, and that the world doesn't revolve around you. Being able to love yourself will allow you to go into any dynamic and know that INDEPENDENT of the outcome, you have yourself and your gifts, and that's a statement on its own.

THE SOLIS
BLUEPRINT

Body Language, Eye-Contact

How do you physically communicate the 3Cs? We have just briefly canvassed the energetic aspect of the 3Cs. This dynamic and engaging energy should underscore all of your communications, slowly bridging the gap between your intimate circles and the average conversation you have in life so that there is no difference.

Physically showing this is also an art form that needs to be mastered. You have likely heard that the eyes are the windows to the soul, and I believe this to be true. Eyes can elicit more information than words often can. Someone's gaze can communicate authenticity, the difference between a lie or the truth, and every spectrum of emotion. Make sure you use them to your advantage. You need to be using eye contact with intent.

There is a subtly to it, something I try not to think too hard about, but something you should ensure that you master. When a recruiter is talking to me, I make sure that **I look directly at them consistently, without breaking eye contact.** You want to show the recruiters that every word that comes out of their mouths is gold— that you are present and curious, engaging with every uttered syllable. Learn to tilt and nod your head inquisitively when they pose something in the hypothetical. When they say something that happened in their own lives with incredulous disbelief, shake your head in disbelief with them, and utter the soft "wow," or "seriously?" alongside their lamentations.

People of all walks of life appreciate being mirrored and heard. Become the relatable person who can understand, empathize, and connect with any monologue pointed your way by a recruiter.

When I AM talking, I try to balance direct eye contact with strategic off-looking. When I am ruminating or recalling a particular event that has occurred to me, as one often does in interview settings, I try to direct my gaze into the distance or to the corner of the room for a momentary reflection, as if I am wrestling with a vast sea of philosophical questions that need to be conquered before I can illicit an

THE SOLIS
BLUEPRINT

answer. Doing this will bolster your authenticity; it won't make you seem rigid. It will pull you away from looking like a creep if you're staring at them throughout the interview. Use your ocular inflections wisely.

The messages you can convey from your eyes downward are equally as powerful. Let's check your posture right now. Right now, you are likely slouched over reading this or lying down. Try to press your lower back into your chair and have both feet planted directly into the floor, equidistant from your shoulders. The best posture advice I ever got was from my younger brother. It's three simple steps:

1. shrug your shoulders up all the way to your ears
2. roll your shoulder blades back
3. drop your shoulders and elbows down.

Maintain this position throughout the entirety of your interview, and you'll feel orders of magnitude more powerful than you would if you were nervously reclused into your chair. Remember, you are worthy of all things you set your mind to, so it's time to start standing like it.

These tips can and should be rehearsed in front of a mirror. You need to know how you look, and as corny of a suggestion it may be, it will genuinely help you feel more ready for the game day if you've formed that mental imprint as to how you speak in interview settings. Another strategy in line with that is to film yourself and unpack the details. How was your posture? Are you using eye contact in an impactful way, or are you darting around the room? Do you look or sound too scripted or robotic?

The last tip is hand gestures and expressions. Some people are very handsy with how they choose to talk. I think hand gestures can be compelling, but they may not come naturally to many people. Hand gestures over Zoom interviews can be awkward, too, since your hands look orders of magnitude larger over a computer camera and may be off-putting to the recruiters. There are likely some great resources you can find to integrate hand gestures into your interviews. My basic

THE SOLIS
BLUEPRINT

interviews. My basic suggestions for in-person interviews are to have your hands clasped on the table in front of you, ready to be used at a moment's notice. Some hand gestures that I use autonomically are the karate chop into flat hand motion when trying to emphasize a realization or point. Another common one that I use is the self-point and chest-tap when I am introspecting on a personality aspect or personal experience. I will gladly discuss some common hand gesture suggestions to augment your interview game in the 1:1 coaching sessions.

Dress for Success

The last section of the interview basics is your attire and presentation. I wanted to leave this for last for obvious reasons. If you cannot muster self-confidence and eye contact, it won't matter if you're dressed to the nines in couture. The quality of the fabric will not redeem you.

Now that we HAVE gotten to this point, let's briefly touch on common sense:

I adhere to a rule of thumb that you should be dressed formally no matter what stage of an interview you are at, whether it is a first-round, final-round, 15 minutes, or 2 hours. Men, this means suit and tie. At the very minimum, a jacket over a buttoned shirt, but the connection is the distinguishing line between something being business casual and business formal. A subtle yet highly impactful addition to your suit game is to add a pocket square with a bit of zest and flair. Keep your ties simple and refined but show the recruiters you are a bit of a left-brain thinker with your colour creativity. For ladies, wearing a jacket and formal skirt is also a great way to elevate the formality of your presence.

Many people underestimate the importance of attire, and others worry about "over-dressing." To that I say nonsense, and I am a firm believer that you cannot overdress for an interview of any sort. Even for firm cultures that pride themselves on being "laidback," always dress formally unless they explicitly tell you not to. The people working in San Francisco in jeans and a tee-shirt earned the ability to do so by securing their job. You haven't earned that privilege yet.

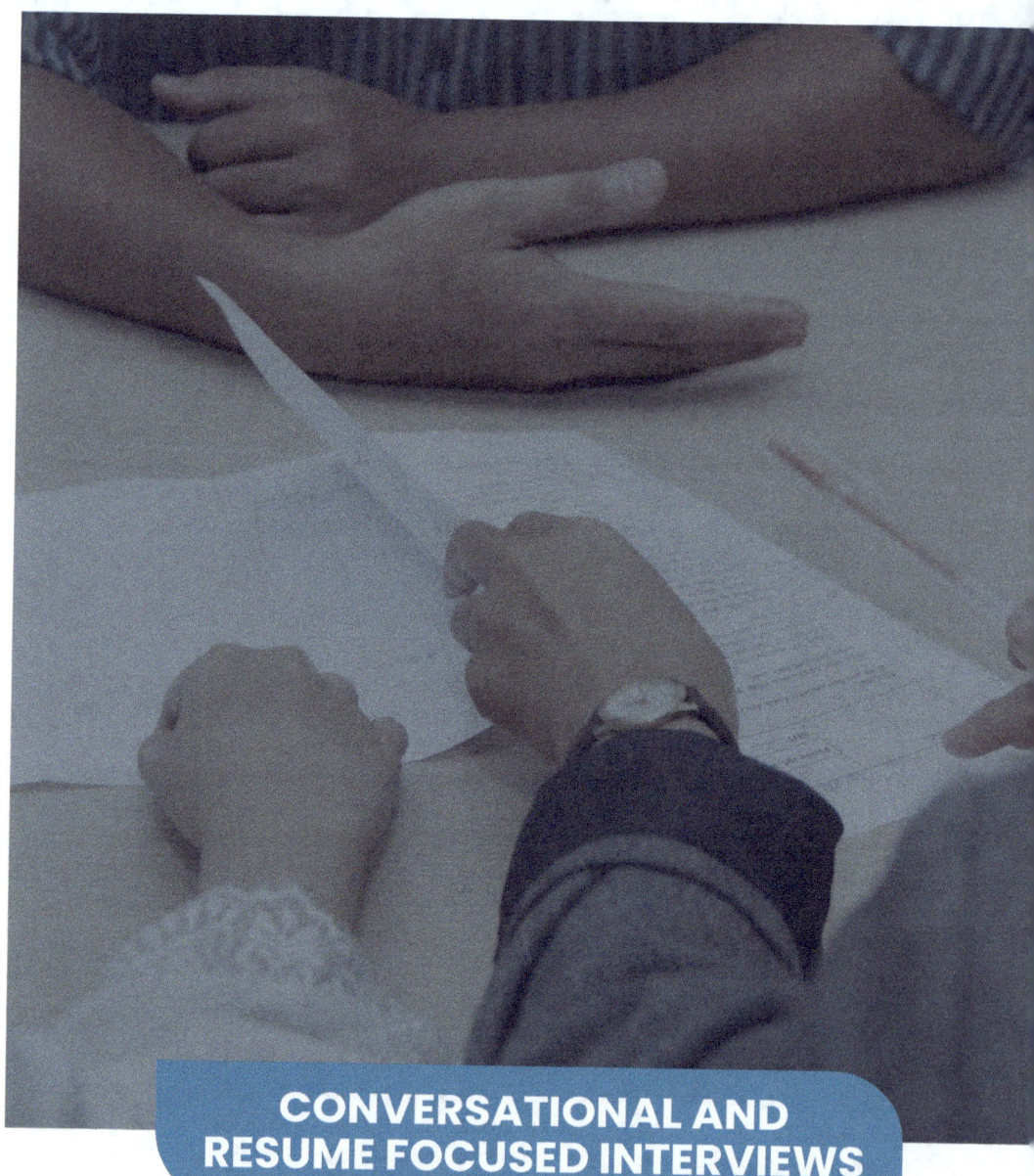

CONVERSATIONAL AND RESUME FOCUSED INTERVIEWS

THE SOLIS BLUEPRINT

Now the good stuff. Conversational and Resume Focused interviews comprise many interview styles that you'll often get when you apply for jobs at law firms or generic corporate jobs. Some of the firms you apply for may prefer a hybrid model of conversational + behavioural (which we will get to). However, pure conversational interviews are the best ones to get.

Conversational interviews are exactly what they sound like: a conversation. Suppose you find yourself in one of these interviews. In that case, chances are the recruiter, on behalf of the firm, is assessing the following information from you:

1. Your "fit" and overall chemistry as it pertains to the firm's culture and chemistry
2. Your experience and how it relates to the firm and job
3. Your ability to adapt to the demands of the firm

It really doesn't get more complicated than that, which is why they're my favourite. It's also why the previous chapter on the 3Cs and your ability to put the best version of yourself forward will be of the utmost importance to knock these out of the park. I will teach you a formulaic way that will allow you to handle ANY deviation or replication of this interview form without any falter.

This method is the golden ticket of this e-book, a technique that I am trying to implore to all my students: The Storyboard Method. Once you've mapped out and visualized how you will use this method, you will truly feel unstoppable. It will literally allow you to handle any question thrown your way with ease. Let's get into it.

The Storyboard Method

I want you to open up your resume and have it in front of you while you read through this section. Like physically, print out your resume, and have a real-life copy in front of you on your desk. Take out another piece of paper and have that paper beside your resume.

THE SOLIS BLUEPRINT

I want you to put the first year of your earliest resume item on the blank piece of paper at the top. For example, if your resume expands as far back as 2016, put 2016 at the top. I then want you to draw an arrow down from 2016 to the bottom of the blank page, and at the bottom of the blank page, I want you to have your current year. It should look something like this:

2016

↓

2022

Looking at that gap between 2016 and 2022, I want you to think of a theme that pops out. Imagine a producer for a TV show approaches you and is tasked with designing a character arc or character development piece exclusively centred around you. The only information they have about you is the experiences listed on your resume. How do you string them all together to tell a story that can be communicated to a TV producer? Write a few bullet points alongside that arrow on your page. Populate the blank space with a few binding terms to fit that storyline.

Is this confusing? Let me break this down for you even more. Let's say I'm applying for a job at a law firm, and again, all they have on me is my resume. Let's build a storyboard that MAKES LOGICAL SENSE as to why I am deserving and ready for this job at this firm. **Let's unpack my life a bit.**

I grew up in a small town (Point A) and studied Biology for my undergraduate degree (Point B), and now I'm studying in law school (Point C). How the hell do I tell a story about that? How does my Point A>Point B> Point C illustrate that I am an ideal candidate? How can I possibly find words that connect small-town jobs to a biology degree to being in law school to now applying for a firm? Well, along the way from A to B to C, I garnered experience, some of which is on my resume:

THE SOLIS
BLUEPRINT

In undergrad, I got really involved in mental health **advocacy** and **leadership**. Before law school, **I travelled** to many countries and **worked abroad** in South America. I taught swimming lessons, landscaped, and worked in **hospitality** with a ton of other people in the **community**.

Now you see that I have more options to work with between A-B-C. You'll also see that I've bolded some word choices. Let's lay those words out:

Advocacy
Leadership
Travel
Working Abroad
Hospitality
Community

What do all of these words elucidate to you about a person? What if you were responsible for designing a show about a character? Let me ask that differently—how do you convert those connecting words into a story?

Well, it shows that herein lies a person who is always drawn to roles of working with people, advocating on behalf of people, and exploring the world to gain new perspectives about people. This is a very people-focused individual. This is the **STORYBOARD**. No matter where and what this person was doing, they were always finding ways to work with people, advocate on behalf of people, and surround themselves with people, whether in hospitality or travelling. THIS IS YOUR UNDERLYING "WHY." This is your home base for answering any questions that come to you in a conversational interview.

If your storyboard theme is "being drawn to people," "being an advocate," "being a team player," or something completely different, you NEED to make sure that all your answers return to this theme, even in the most casual of conversations.

Let's walk through a few scenarios together.

THE SOLIS BLUEPRINT

Say in the interview when they ask you (not if, but when they ask you), what draws you to the position, or why you are applying to the position, you should be readily thinking of your storyboard. You should also consider what the job description requires or some central tenants of the position. Let's return to our law firm example. Working at a law firm requires working with people, solving complex problems, and looking to advocate on behalf of people.

In answering this question, I'd start with a mock script that would sound like this:

> "I've been very drawn to this _____[firm] in particular because I've been looking for a firm that shares the same values of community connection and customer service that I've fostered in my own life. As someone who has spent 10 years in mental health advocacy and customer service more generally, I know the importance of being able to foster relationships and build working dynamics with individuals who you seek to advocate and represent. My time at [REFERENCE A POINT ON YOUR RESUME THAT IS RELATED TO FIRM VALUE] was eye-opening for me in allowing me to realize that I thrive in settings that allow me to have a working relationship with clients, as well as direct mentorship and guidance; both things I know that your firm prioritizes.
>
> I know that [firm name] is comprised of a team of people that work hard, regularly solve complex problems on behalf of clients, and also actively gives back to the Community. This really resonates with me, and I truly believe that my experiences mesh well with your firm culture and values."

As you'll see, I was able to plant a seed of perceived alignment in the recruiter's head. I've mentioned to them that not only can I see myself in their firm, but that my experiences mesh with their entire mission statement as an organization. Always revert to your storyboard themes when asked any question. If you are familiar with your story, the narrative you are trying to communicate about yourself, and the reason that everything you have done in your life has cumulated to this exact moment in your interview, you can answer anything.

THE SOLIS
BLUEPRINT

A tip that is imperative to your performance is to never, under any circumstances, sound scripted or come off as if you are trying to memorize something rote from your brain. Even in the above script, it is up to you to mold the listed experiences to match yours and ensure that you can match the speaking style to your own cadence, expressions, mannerisms, etc.

How To Answer The 'Classic' Questions in Conversational Interviews

When you sign up for our coaching services, we're also going to include a PDF document when you sign up that contains over 50 of the most common interview questions that you can expect to see in a conversational and behavioural interview setting. We'll also teach you how to answer these questions in the call. More on that when you sign up.

There are a staple set of questions that you should have an answer almost prepared for in your head for any interview that you walk into. We'll go over the almost guaranteed three questions that you'll get. Now that we know how to "storyboard" our answers and structure our responses, let's dive into a few of them.

Tell us about yourself?

One of the most fundamental questions that every interview style will likely start with is the "Tell us about yourself?" question. Contrary to what you may have been told, there is undoubtedly a correct way to answer this question. This question is the question that sets the stage for the remainder of the conversational interview. Often a lot of what you provide in this answer will be followed up on by the recruiter if it sounds interesting, captivating, or applicable. You must leverage the likelihood of receiving a follow-up question from the recruiter by meticulously building an alluring storyline.

THE SOLIS BLUEPRINT

A great framework to operate from is the following:

1. Summary of your current position
2. Storyline of how you got to your current position
3. What traits and skills encompass your personality
4. Why this job is the next most logical step for you with all that in mind.

Let's build this out into a proper answer:

"Well, my name is ___, and I'm currently working at [firm], right now as a junior level associate. My responsibilities here include analyzing files, client intake, and regularly assisting my supervisors on an array of public facing tasks. My path of actually getting to [firm] and the realm of law more generally has been a direct extension of things that I've always loved doing. I'm someone who has always had a passion and interest in working with people and advocacy more generally. Whether that was working at my local pool in Aquatics, managing teams and conferences, or playing varsity sports, I am somebody who has always found myself naturally drawn to environments that allow me to solve problems in a team setting and apply my passion for working with people to the greater good. My friends and colleagues would tell you that I am an extremely hard worker, someone who is the first one in and last one out, and also one of the worst players at golf, and that I become hyper fixated on the things that I am passionate about. Outside of these things, I am huge outdoors fanatic, and I am terrible at golf."

This is a reliable and solid framework that has paid dividends for me in my experiences with interviewing. I have even had a Partner at a reputable firm respond to that opening answer by telling me how good of a sales pitch it was. With any answer, it's crucial to adopt your own experiences, cadence and speaking style.

A critical mistake that people make in answering their questions is thinking that the recruiter/interviewers just want to hear your resume recapped and summarized. Here's a hint: they don't. Why would they? They presumably have read your resume

THE SOLIS BLUEPRINT

and likely already have it in front of them.

Tell us about your most recent job?

The key to answering this question is to create an air of direct applicability and connection to the job that you are seeking to your most recent job. This question can be answered very strongly and conversely very poorly.

A very mediocre answer to this question would be simply reciting the job description and your job duties and calling it a day. While you may be "technically" answering the question being asked of you, it is not what they are trying to flesh out in posing that question. A recruiter is looking for transferability of your skills and experience, pertinent exposure to tasks that may be expected of you in the new job, and general fit.

The way to answer this question is to be prepared in advance and know the qualities, duties, and responsibilities of the position of interest. An excellent way to figure this out is to start reaching out to other people in the job you're applying for well before the interview. This will allow you to better understand the position's expectations. Once you know this, you can strategically whittle down your most recent experience to sound like it is a direct, perfectly aligned fit and logical extension to the position that you are applying for.

Even if your most recent job was a garbageman or sanitation worker and you are now applying for a consulting job, you should be able to reduce and redress the skills to make them directly applicable. Let's work with this example: you are applying for a consulting position. Although consulting interviews are their own format, suppose this consulting firm asks you to explain your most recent position as a sanitation worker for your city. How do you bridge these two completely distinct fields of work in an answer?

Firstly, from your research and conversations with current consultants, you should know that a consulting job requires immense problem-solving skills, the ability to

THE SOLIS BLUEPRINT

work under strict deadlines, and voluminous teamwork. When you are inevitably asked to describe your most recent job, you can word it to be something like this:

> "My current job with [x] has been an incredible experience. I am responsible for maintaining the city's wastewater and sanitation systems, and regularly work alongside various stakeholders and officers to ensure hygienic compliance with all of our operations. Most of my work has been done under tight deadlines, and I am very familiar with working long-hours. I have a job that an entire population depends on me for, so I am very familiar with how to work under pressure and respond quickly to my clients' needs. I regularly was faced with roadblocks such as faulty pipes and infrastructure issues that I had to fall back and consult with my team members on. **I know that all of these experiences are similar to the skills that are demanded of a consultant, and it is part of the reason as to why I am drawn to [x firm]"**

The bolded text serves to remind you that you should constantly be circling back to the WHY factor for the job you are applying for. Although reducing your current job to its transferable skills remains the most important task, the cherry on top is ending with a statement of how said skills have primed you to be the most ideal candidate for the job. In our coaching programs, we're going to actually sit down with you 1:1 and build out your answers to all of these questions, but for now this can serve as a great framework to aid you.

Why should we hire you?

The last of the capstone questions is the "why should we hire you?" question. This question can often be synonymized with other variations such as "why do you want this job?" or "what about you makes you ideal for this role, etc. Your response to this question can be a definite game-changer in the interview and certainly can boost your chances if a recruiting panel is torn between you and another set of candidates.

Answering this question is a matter of your confidence, the importance of which I have already mentioned at nauseum in the former chapter. Nailing this question

THE SOLIS
BLUEPRINT

on the head will literally come down to how confidently you can convince the recruiter that it would be a mistake not to hire you given your personality, your experience, your energy, and your aura

You will typically have an advantage in answering this question, given how it is almost always at the end of an interview, wherein you have already spent time with the recruiter and provided (hopefully) enough information on your past experiences and skills that this question will be a breeze. If this question is right out of the gate, I suggest answering it like the "tell us about yourself" question. Again, I don't think this is likely to happen; I have never encountered it in my interviews, and I think it's a terrible way to kick off a conversation.

I tackle this question in the following framework:
1. Remind the recruiter of all your experiences and skills that you have gone over
2. Convince the recruiter that said skills are a perfect fit for the job and the company
3. End on a note of mentioning you wanting to build a career or life in said profession, and 'x' company is a perfect place to do so.
4. "You won't regret it."

Let's look at how that sounds in an actual answer:

THE SOLIS BLUEPRINT

> *"I think one thing that should jump out about my resume and the conversation that we've had is that I am someone who has always been drawn to roles of advocacy, teamwork, and problem solving. I am someone who not only knows how to build lasting relationships with individuals, but I am also someone who can provide tangible solutions and lasting outcomes for those who rely on my skillset. I think that hiring me would be an excellent addition to your team and the mission that you are already pursuing, and that is providing the best possible service and solutions to those who seek your help. I am confident that my drive, work-ethic, ability to learn and grow, and personability would be a great fit for your team. As someone who is looking to springboard myself into a career that is centred around client-driven advocacy, I am certain that [x firm] is the perfect place for me to start/continue, and I am confident that you will not regret hiring me"*

Re-read that answer and see if you can spot how the framework was applied in that answer. Regardless of your experience, it is always good to throw in a few buzzwords that recruiters love to hear—advocacy, client-driven service, teamwork, etc. However, it is crucial that you do not underestimate the importance of knowing the skillset that comprises the job you are applying for. Make sure you come in over-prepared and over-knowledgeable to mold the above answer perfectly into what they want.

How To Answer The 'Casual' Questions

The last component of a conversational style interview is the casual conversation that should hopefully ensue in the interview itself. What separates conversational interviews from behavioural is that most of your questions outside the above-structured ones will be simple questions about various points of your resume.

Again, it is essential to have a languages, skills, or interest section on your resume. It increases the likelihood that a recruiter will find something that resonates with their own interests (a massive win if this happens!). Handling casual questions that are rooted around your resume points should be dealt with the same framework of

THE SOLIS
BLUEPRINT

the "tell us about your most recent job experience," wherein you should be able to distill and reduce the skills and convey the experience in a way that is directly relevant to the job that you are applying to.

Above all, you must be able to have fun during these interviews. While being instructed to "have fun" during a stressful job interview seems oxymoronic, it truly is one of the best pieces of advice that I've received. Interviewers are really assessing you for fit and chemistry. You will be in excellent hands if you can exude a persona that demonstrates that you are calm and yourself under stressful moments.

BEHAVIOURAL INTERVIEWS

THE SOLIS BLUEPRINT

Given the format's structured component and unpredictable nature, this interview style and subsequent questions often throw off candidates the most. We have all been there—you're chatting, getting settled into the interview, and then the recruiter asks a question that comes off so formal and rigid that your mind draws a blank and you fumble. While I wish that every interview could be a conversational style, I will walk you through the skeleton of behavioural interviews and show you that they are just as, if not slightly easier, to prepare for than conversational interviews.

Preparation

While preparation is undoubtedly an underlying theme for so many of the previous chapters, it is undoubtedly the most important and crucial element in ensuring success for the behavioural interview. Given how so many of the behavioural interview questions are centred around soft skills and practical experience, it is in your best interests to make sure you can describe scenarios and stories from the following areas of your resume:

1. A time you had to resolve a conflict
2. A time you had a disagreement with a team member
3. A time you had a disagreement with a manager
4. A time you worked with an uncooperative client or customer
5. A time you failed/made a mistake
6. What your proudest accomplishment on your resume is
7. What your proudest accomplishment off your resume is
8. A time you had to solve a complex problem in a situation you were unfamiliar with
9. A time you had to manage many competing deadlines under tight timelines
10. A time you had to think on your feet

I assure you, if you can have a story or example to provide that can answer those 10 questions, you will be able to answer nearly any behavioural question that comes your way. Almost all behavioural questions will be those questions or derivatives of those questions. In fact, I can simplify this even more. Recruiters want to hear the applicability of your resume experience and skills in the following realms:

THE SOLIS BLUEPRINT

1. Teamwork
2. Conflict Resolution
3. Problem Solving and Creativity
4. Time Management and Work Ethic
5. Communicability with Colleagues and Clients

When you sign up for our coaching program, we will provide you with a list of over 50+ behavioural questions and walk you through each one before your interview so that you literally will be able to handle anything that comes your way. In other words, we will literally sculpt all of your resume points to match all of the above questions. Regardless, having your stories and scenarios picked out for each of the above 10 will be a great start to your prep.

How do you choose which story or resume point to choose when prepping your answers? The first thing I suggest is to make sure you have diversity in your pool of answers. Don't make 5/10 answers stem from your most recent experience or one point on your resume. I have done this in a law firm interview, and I am almost certain it was my demise. It demonstrated one-dimensionality and a lack of well-roundedness. Don't make this mistake. Have a diverse spread of answers and content to pull from. This definitely includes the most recent job experience you have but should also include your hobbies, sports experiences, travel, and other jobs. Suppose you played varsity sports or worked in an insanely busy restaurant. In that case, those can be great fodder to build an answer to time management or teamwork questions. Only you know your resume and what it entails; however, we will build out your behavioural interview plan when you sign up for the coaching services.

Now that you have your stories planned and ready to fire off at the drop of a dime, we need to figure out how to dissect and structure them into captivating responses. Enter the STAR method.

THE SOLIS BLUEPRINT

The STAR Method

The STAR method is certainly not mine. It is an extremely common method that many career coaches and blogs will teach you. In my opinion, it is simple yet effective. The STAR method stands for:
- Story/Scenario
- Task
- Action
- Results

The STAR method will be your backboard that you should be falling back on for every single behavioural question that comes your way. As you can see now, having your stories prepared is exceptionally applicable here. What we now want to do is be able to distill the facts to their core components. When you're telling your stories, you must be only telling the absolute vital facts that align with the answer you are going to give. The recruiter doesn't need to know your former manager's name or what your office ordered for Friday team lunches. Keep it distilled.

Let's say you have been asked the "tell us about a time you worked with an uncooperative client?" question. You think back to the story that you have eloquently prepared, and you recall that you have worked with an uncooperative client. Here is the level of detail you should include to satisfy the 'S' prong.

"My former job as a client support specialist at 123 Insurance required me to regularly work with clients in highly emotional situations, actively working to mitigate client's concerns with responsive solutions. One incident in particular required me to support a client who had lost all of his family's documentation in a house fire, so you can imagine the level of emotional inflammation that was present in the call right off the bat."

THE SOLIS
BLUEPRINT

As you can see from that answer, I have not only snuck in a few bullet points of job duties and responsibilities, but I have also distilled an entire story to its most basic facts: an extremely simplified version of what the job was, and what the problem I was faced with that is pertinent to the question being asked. 'S' is now satisfied.

For Task, you want to take the same approach as above: distill and reduce your responsibilities into something short and captivating. **A trick here is to reduce the responsibilities into buzzwords that are synonymous with the job you are currently applying for.** If you are applying for a sales job that will require active engagement with the public, we're going to make sure that exact phrase is thrown in your summary of your task. Let's go back to 123 Insurance and sculpt an example:

"In this role, I regularly engaged with diverse cross-sections of the public and was tasked with mitigating client pain points and providing tailor-made solutions unique to each client's problem."

Here we have sprinkled a few buzzwords from the job posting into the answer, and now your menial task sounds a lot more suited to the job description. You handle an array of clients with different needs, learn to adapt your solutions to their problems and ensure uniqueness in your approach. Short and effective. Now for the most critical point, the actual action that you took.

For any question that you get that pertains to diffusing a heated situation or butting heads with another person, the golden answer that you provide should center around your ability to listen to opposing perspectives, empathize with opposing views, and be able to make the other person feel heard. This is a solid framework that can never go wrong. I've even said something like, "most of the time, people who are frustrated with you don't even want a solution in the moment; they just want to be heard," and I have found that clause has been very well received.

In answering your 'Action,' you could then say:

THE SOLIS
BLUEPRINT

"I knew how emotionally tolling this event must have been on the client, so I gave him all the time and space to communicate his problem to me, I made sure that he felt understood and completely empathized with, ensuring that he knew that I was aware of the gravity of the situation. **I believe this is crucial to navigating all disagreements and something that I actively deploy.** *After he felt heard and understood, I proposed a solution."*

Your action piece should elucidate that you are aware of what steps work in those situations. Prove that this was not a one-time thing but something that you regularly deploy in your day-to-day life, something that is almost second nature.

In answering your 'Result,' this is where you drive it home. You make sure that you make the result sound like a perfect, direct outcome of your action and something that you can replicate and transfer to the job you are applying to.

"I not only was able to communicate a solution for the client through an emotionally tolling ordeal, but I was also able to retain this customer for a future policy plan, and also get referred to his family members **given the respect, patience, and empathy that I deployed with him,** *and my other clients more generally.* **This is a lesson that I now regularly deploy in my dealings with clients."**

A great touch to your result section is demonstrating that you have that perspective to look back on an experience and identify that not only was it not just a fluke or a 'one-off' incident but is now part and parcel of your toolkit of skills that you regularly use to handle similar situations. This will demonstrate to your recruiter that said scenario should, in theory, be directly applicable to the new job should you be faced with similar circumstances.

Deal-Sealing Methods

The STAR method should be your go-to framework to answer all your behavioural questions and is something that you should be prepared for before your interviews. In fact, I suggest that students write out a STAR chart on a piece of paper to

THE SOLIS
BLUEPRINT

prepare for the most predictable forms of questions you can expect. Using the STAR method and subsequently preparing for your behavioural interview with STAR prep is a great way to ensure your success. Still, you can also use other techniques to bolster your chances.

Multi-Pot Answers

A strategy I used in my STAR method was how I slightly modify my 'S' and my 'R' answer to include more than one experience in my answer. I call this the Multi-Pot method. This method shows the recruiters that you hail from multidimensional experiences. You had the opportunity to learn and apply various soft skills with success in different settings, thereby further demonstrating that you are consistent in my execution of said skills.

The Multi-Pot method is a subtle addition to your existing STAR framework. Still, you are going to 'name drop' other instances and responsibilities **very briefly** that overlap with the soft skill you are trying to showcase. If this sounds confusing, let me show you an example from 123 Insurance that also inserts the Multi-Pot method. Pay attention to the **bolded words**.

THE SOLIS
BLUEPRINT

> "I've been fortunate to work in many capacities that involve solving problems for clients, be that my time as a marketing intern for ABC Marketing, or even working as a lifeguard in my local pool. My former job as a client support specialist at 123 Insurance required me to regularly work with clients in highly emotional situations, actively working to mitigate client's concerns with responsive solutions. One incident in particular required me to support a client who had lost all of his family's documentation in a house fire, so you can imagine the level of emotional inflammation that was present in the call right off the bat...........
>
> [R] I not only was able to communicate a solution for the client through an emotionally tolling ordeal, but I was also able to retain this customer for a future policy plan, and also get referred to his family members given the respect, patience, and empathy that I deployed with him, and my other clients more generally. This is an approach that I have used in all my interactions with clients, be that at a pool, or as a marketing intern, and is something that I believe to be highly applicable to your company."

From here, you should be able to see how in a few extra seconds, you have gone from a unidimensional experience to proving that your problem-solving skills intersect with numerous experiences that you've been directly involved in. The last sentence in the above box underlined is a compelling addition that I suggest you always cap your STAR answers with, which is a trick called mirroring.

Regardless of the soft skill, you can always refer back to the job in question and remind them that your mastery of that skill is directly applicable to the job at hand. Again, having the pre-emptive research completed of the job you are applying for will make your mirroring even better. Instead of leaving a sentence at "...is something that I believe to be highly applicable to your company" you can say, "is something that I believe to be highly applicable here given your commitment and direct exposure that your sales associates have with clients and the general public."

Adding the Multi-Pot and Mirroring strategies are sure-fire ways to take your A-level answers to an A+.

CASE INTERVIEWS

THE SOLIS BLUEPRINT

Overview

Simply put, a case interview is the analysis of a business question. Unlike most other interview questions, it is an interactive process that allows for freedom of creativity and strategy. As the candidate, you are tasked with conducting insightful dialogue with the interviewer to understand the business to make a detailed recommendation. The majority of case interviewers don't require a specific answer. This allows candidates to best distinguish themselves with their creativity, knowledge, and critical thinking. The interviewer is looking for a thought process that demonstrates your "out-of-the-box" thinking and strategic thinking to analyze problems and strategize solutions. Most candidates fear they need specific knowledge of the industry to excel; however, the most fundamental aspect is staying calm under pressure and being both articulate and analytical at the same time. These cases are interactive, scenario-based discussions that are often based on actual projects the interviewer has worked on or current scenarios or challenges clients of the interviewer have presented. Many other employers outside of management consulting also use case interviews. Still, this guide will focus on the most common management consulting format. Consulting case interviews for the likes of BCG serve as the gold standard for case interviews.

Expectations and What Firms Look For

Preparation and adaptability are the keys to unlocking success in a case interview. They expect that you have not only familiarity with a case interview structure but that you've practiced and are familiar with what to expect. This preparedness shows you are proactive and diligent, which is a vital characteristic of any successful consultant. Overall during the process of a case interview, the candidate is expected to display the following abilities and traits:
- Take notes and summarize key points
- Understand the issue; ask clarifying questions as needed
- Identify the underlying assumptions, ambiguity, and gaps
- Summarize specific issues/findings and synthesize information to draw conclusions

THE SOLIS BLUEPRINT

- Solve complex problems with a logical and structured, hypothesis-driven approach
- State recommendations, outline next steps and expected project results/impacts

THE CASE

Generally, most case interview scenarios are cases that require you to analyze a company (the client) and cases that ask you to explore the market/industry. In tackling each, there is an approach of core questions you should be asking about the company and market. These questions will allow you to contextualize and structure your approach. It will enable you to be more efficient and effective with your synthesis of all key information and ensure that you don't miss anything critical. Leverage and memorize the following questions so that they become second nature when you are reading through or being presented a case. You should learn these to the point where you are actively generating answers to these as debrief on all the information presented within the case.

Core questions to memorize:

- CCC (Customer, Company, Competition)
  - Who are the customers (e.g., individual consumers or business clients?)
  - What are their primary criteria for purchasing?
  - What are the company's strengths and weaknesses?
  - What is their core business?
  - What is the customer segmentation, and what are their characteristics and changing needs?
  - Profitability by customer and product segment?
  - What is the market share, and who are the main competitors?
  - Cannibalization between products?
  - Production capabilities/capacity, and what are the distribution and supply chain channels?

THE SOLIS BLUEPRINT

- Profit = Revenues - Costs
  - What are the major revenue streams, and what percentage of the total revenue does each stream represent?
  - What are the company's major costs, expenses, and investments?
  - What are the sum volumes of price, where the price varies by the segment it serves?
  - What are the costs and revenues relative to competitors and the industry?
  - What is the ROE (profit margin x inventory turns x financial leverage)
  - Profit margin = earnings / sales
  - Inventory turns = sales / assets
  - Financial leverage = assets / shareholder equity

Various Frameworks

Frameworks are only a tool to guide your approach. Most business schools teach these frameworks, and you can easily find guides on leveraging each online. The interviewer will be aware when applying a framework; however, be cautious in basing your complete approach around a framework. The best approach is to leverage a framework as a foundation to assess the case and use your unique analytical and deductive reasoning skills to creatively build your approach and recommendations. Use frameworks sparingly, and do not force them as a solution to tackling the case as they can sometimes be inappropriately applied.

THE SOLIS BLUEPRINT

Framework	Definition	When to use
M&A Framework	Mergers & Acquisitions	Evaluate a potential acquisition
Porters Five Forces	Supplier Power, Buyer Power, Threat of New Entry, Threat of Substitution, Competitive Rivalry	Evaluating Industry Profitability
Profit Tree	Profit = Revenues - Costs	Evaluate Profitability Issues
4 C's	Customer, Competition, Cost, Capabilities	New Product to Market
Business Situation Framework (3 C's 1 P)	Customer, Competition, Company and Product	Evaluative a Company's Situation Qualitatively
4 P's	Price, Product Position/Place, Promotions	Evaluating the Market
Seven S's Framework	Strategy, Structure, Systems, Shared Values, Skills, Style, Staf	Evaluate Internals of a company
Rule of 72	Indicates roughly how long it will take for an investment to double.	72/Interest Rate = Number of Years Doubled

Case Structure and Approach

While interviews may vary widely with each company and industry, there are some aspects of a case that you'll come across frequently. You can apply the same approach when preparing as this generalized structure and framework can be used in most cases. The classic and most common type of case interview is the business case, in which you're presented with a business scenario and asked to analyze it and make recommendations. These can be shown in a handout, presentation, verbally, or in some cases, within a group format. Nonetheless, you can apply the same core steps to succeed in any case interview format.

Concluding Remarks

The world of interview prep contains a vast, seemingly infinite pool of resources and opinions that often can feel overwhelming to attempt to navigate. With so many coaches, gurus, and purported experts in the space of interview prep, it is no surprise that so many students feel uncertain about the best approach to take when handling an upcoming job interview.

This book was never meant to be an isolated guide on its own but rather a supplement that can accompany you through whatever interview process you choose to follow. As two students who have handled over 50 interviews combined in our own lives, we are confident that at least some of the information in this guide can be useful to you for whatever you choose to apply it for.

Interviewing is as much of a skill as it is an art and is something that truly does need adequate preparation and practice to master. It is a muscle that must be flexed and trained to maximize your potential. Part of the inspiration for writing this guide was that amidst the abundance of all the resources on the internet, very few, if not any, discussed or mentioned the importance of possessing the three Cs: confidence, charisma, and character. As I mentioned in earlier chapters, you can walk into an interview with a perfectly designed script made by MBAs and Harvard Business students that purportedly will guarantee you any job you see fit. You can even go in with the script written by an AI computer. However, if you cannot look your recruiter in the eye, know how to use your hands and body language to your advantage, and learn how to apply your storyboard to the job description, I have bad news for you. No amount of scripting or preparation will get you that job. It is why that half of this guide is focused on the importance of developing your personal side.

Although we will not guarantee 100% success of you acquiring a job that you were applying for, should you choose to engage in our coaching programs, I can assure you that we will be treating your resume, your cover letter, and your interview prep as if it was our own. The dedication you will receive in this coaching program will ensure that every cent you invest in this program will be directly invested back into your future with the utmost commitment to your growth.

We can't wait to see where you go.

Solis Coaching

www.ingramcontent.com/pod-product-compliance
Lightning Source LLC
Chambersburg PA
CBHW070311220526
45465CB00004B/1837